HOW TO
FOCUS
THICH NHAT HANH

**PARALLAX
PRESS**

BERKELEY, CALIFORNIA

Parallax Press
2236B Sixth Street
Berkeley, California 94710
parallax.org

Parallax Press is the publishing division of
Plum Village Community of Engaged Buddhism
© 2022 Plum Village Community of Engaged
Buddhism, Inc.
Printed in Canada on 100% postconsumer recycled paper

Cover and text design by Debbie Berne
Illustrations © 2022 by Jason DeAntonis

The material in this book comes from previously
published books and articles by Thich Nhat Hanh.

The Sixteen Exercises of Mindful Breathing,
pages 85–125, follow the order found in Samyukta
Agama 803 rather than that found in the Pali version,
Majjhima Nikaya 118.

ISBN: 978-1-952692-17-8
E-book ISBN: 978-1-946764-93-5

Library of Congress Control Number: 2022936119

2 3 4 5 / 26 25 24 23 22

CONTENTS

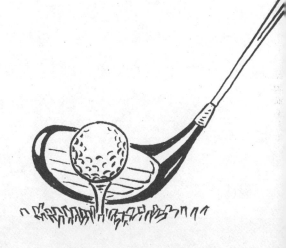

NOTES ON FOCUSING

The river must be calm
to reflect the full moon.

The clear mind has insight into
the true nature of things.

ATTENTION AND HAPPINESS ARE CONNECTED

Mindfulness is the miracle that can restore wholeness to our dispersed mind, calling it back so we can live fully each moment of life.

Mindfulness always brings concentration, and concentration brings insight.

When you drink your cup of tea, if you are concentrated and you focus your attention on it, then the cup of tea becomes a great joy for you. Mindfulness and concentration bring about not only insight but happiness as well.

CONCENTRATION BRINGS UNDERSTANDING

The more mindful we are, the more concentrated we are. The word for concentration in Sanskrit, *samādhi*, means *steadiness*, *non-interruption*, *not wavering*. The object of your concentration may be a cloud, a flower, or your anger. If your focus dies, and sometime later is born again, it's not concentration. In the state of concentration, you keep your focus steady, even, and continuous. When our mindfulness and concentration are powerful, we can make a breakthrough and get an insight. Insight brings understanding and has the power to liberate us from ignorance, discrimination, craving, fear, anger, and despair.

TOUCHING LIFE DEEPLY

You can enjoy every moment of your daily life when you have mindfulness and concentration. When I walk mindfully from one place to another, I enjoy my in-breath, my out-breath, and my steps. When you are concentrated, you sink deeply into what is there. When you contemplate a flower, you get in touch very profoundly with the flower, which is a wonder of life.

When you hold your cup of tea and enjoy it, you get in touch deeply with your tea and enjoy the peace, joy, and freedom that is offered to you by drinking tea. Freedom is our practice. If you have some freedom and solidity brought to you by mindfulness and concentration, peace and joy are possible.

RETURNING TO OURSELVES

In everyday life we are often lost in forgetfulness. Our mind chases after thousands of
things, and we rarely take the time to come
back to ourselves. When we have been lost
in forgetfulness for a long time, we lose
touch with ourselves and feel alienated from
ourselves. Conscious breathing is a marvelous
way to return to ourselves. When we are aware
of our breath, we come back to ourselves as
quick as a flash of lightning. Like a child who
returns home after a long journey, we feel the
warmth of our hearth, and we find ourselves
again. To come back to ourselves like that is
already a remarkable success on the path of
mindfulness, concentration, and insight.

TOUCHING THE WONDERS OF LIFE

With conscious breathing we come in contact
with life in the present moment—the only
moment when we can touch life. When you
focus your attention on your breath, you find
out very quickly that you are a living reality,
present here and now, sitting on this beautiful
planet Earth. Around you there are trees,
sunshine, and blue sky. Mindfulness and concentration bring you in touch with the wonders
of life and allow you to value and treasure
these things.

FREEDOM FROM REGRET
AND ANXIETY

To breathe with full awareness is a
miraculous way to untie the knots of regret and
anxiety and to come back to life in the present
moment. If we're imprisoned by regrets about
the past, anxiety for the future, or attachment
and aversion in the present, we're not free to
be in contact with life. We're not really living
our life. When we breathe in and out and
follow our breath with attention all the way
through from the beginning to the end, we're
already at ease, no longer dominated by our
anxieties and longings. As we breathe with full
awareness, our breath becomes slower and
more regular; peace and joy arise and become
more stable with every moment. Relying on our
breathing, we come back to ourselves and are
able to restore the oneness of our body and

mind and become whole again. When body and mind are together, we are fully present, fully alive, and able to be in real contact with what is happening in the present moment.

FOCUSING BEGINS WITH THE BREATH

We make our breathing the first object of our concentrated mind. We put all our attention on our breath, so that mind and breath become one. After first focusing on the breath, we can then practice focusing on other phenomena. When we use our breathing to bring all the energy of mind consciousness to one point, our confusion stops, and we are able to sustain the energy of our mind on one object. As we continue to practice, the energy of concentration helps us penetrate deeply into the heart of the object of our focus, and we gain insight and understanding.

AWARENESS OF FEELINGS

We can speak of feelings as being pleasant,
painful, or neutral. Practicing meditation, we
discover how interesting it is to look into our
neutral feelings. As we sit on the grass with
our mind elsewhere, we may have a neutral
feeling. But when we bring our awareness
to the neutral feeling, we find that it's really
quite wonderful to be sitting on the grass in
the sunshine. As we observe the river of our
feelings with mindfulness and concentration,
we find that many neutral feelings are actually
quite pleasant.

MAKING DECISIONS

When there is anxiety, irritation, or anger in us, we cannot decide clearly what to do. When you come back to yourself and breathe mindfully, your mind's attention has only one object: your breath. If you continue to breathe in and out mindfully, you maintain that state of presence and freedom. Your mind will be clearer and you will make better decisions. It's much better to make a decision when your mind is like that rather than when it is in the sway of fear, anger, unclear thinking, and worry.

STOPPING

Meditation has two aspects: *stopping* and *looking deeply*. We tend to stress the importance of looking deeply because it can bring us insight and liberate us from suffering and afflictions. But the practice of stopping is fundamental. Stopping is the very beginning of the practice of meditation. If we cannot stop, we cannot have insight. We have to learn the art of stopping—stopping our thinking, our habit energies, our forgetfulness, and the strong emotions that rule us. When an emotion rushes through us like a storm, we have no peace. We turn on the TV and then we turn it off. We pick up a book and then we put it down.

How can we stop this state of agitation? We can stop by practicing mindful breathing, mindful walking, and deep looking in order to understand. When we are mindful, touching deeply the present moment, the fruits are always understanding, acceptance, love, and the desire to relieve suffering and bring joy.

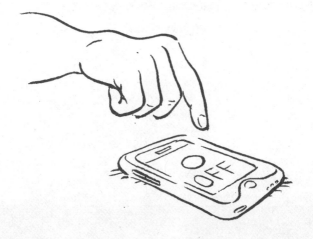

A CLEAR MIND

Meditation is not to avoid problems or run away from difficulties. We do not practice to escape. We practice to have enough strength to confront problems effectively. To do this, we must be calm, fresh, and solid. That is why we need to practice the art of stopping. When we learn to stop, we become calmer, and our mind becomes clearer, like clear water after the particles of mud have settled.

WALKING IN FREEDOM

It is possible to enjoy every step you make at any time you want, whenever you feel the need to move from one place to another, no matter how short the distance. If you make five steps, then make those five steps into a walking meditation. Every step will bring you joy and stability.

When you climb the stairs, climb each step in mindfulness, concentration, and joy. In that way you are doing exactly what the Buddha was doing: generating and transferring your best to the world. Peace, happiness, brotherhood and sisterhood become a reality if we know how to live our daily life in mindfulness and concentration. Invest 100 percent of yourself in the walking. Become aware of every step. It's *you* who are consciously walking. Your habitual preoccupations and ways of thinking are not pulling you away. You retain your sovereignty. You are the one who decides. You walk because it is your intention to walk, and in every step you have freedom. You take each step purposefully, and each mindful step brings you in touch with the wonders of life that are available in the here and now.

This is why, when you are walking, you do not think. If you think, the thinking will steal your walking from you. You don't talk, because talking will take the walking away from you. Walking like this is a pleasure. When mindfulness and concentration are alive in you, you are fully yourself. You don't lose yourself. You walk with grace and dignity. Without mindfulness, you may think of walking as an imposition, a chore. With mindfulness, you see walking as life.

As you walk, let your steps follow the rhythm of your breath. Let your breathing be natural. Breathing in, if your lungs want two steps, then take two steps; if your lungs want three steps then give yourself three steps. Breathing out, you may want to take a step or two more than you did when breathing in. Listen to your lungs. Even if your surroundings are full of noise and agitation, you can still walk in rhythm with your breathing. Even in the commotion of a big city, you can walk with peace, happiness, and an inner smile. Every step should be enjoyable.

RADIO NST

Most of us have a radio constantly playing
in our head, tuned to Radio NST: "Non-Stop
Thinking." Most of this thinking is unproductive.
The more we think, the less available we are
to what is around us. Our mind is filled with
noise, and that's why we can't hear the call of
life. Our heart is calling us, but we don't hear
it. We don't have the time to listen to our heart.
We have to learn to turn off the radio and stop
our thinking, our internal discourse, in order to
be able to fully enjoy the present moment and
live our life.

Our mindful breathing and steps are able to
pull us out of our thinking and bring back the
joy in being alive.

HABIT ENERGY

We may have the will to stop, but our habit
energies are often stronger than our will. Habit
energy is called *vāsanā* in Sanskrit. It is very
important to recognize our habit energy. This
energy may have been transmitted to us by
many generations of ancestors, and we continue to cultivate it. It is very powerful. We are
intelligent enough to know that if we do this or
say that, we will damage our relationship. Yet
when the time comes, we do or say it anyway.
Why? Because our habit energy is stronger
than we are. It is pushing us all the time. Even
if you want to stop, it doesn't allow you to stop.
We say and do things we don't want to, and
afterward we regret it. We make ourselves
and others suffer, and we bring about a lot of
damage. We vow not to do it again, but we do it

again, because our habit energies push us. We need the energy of mindfulness to recognize and be present with our habit energy in order to stop this course of destruction.

With mindfulness we have the capacity to recognize the habit energy every time it manifests. We can say, "Hello, my habit energy, I know you are there!" If we just smile to it, it will lose much of its strength. Mindfulness and concentration are the energies that allow us to recognize our habit energy and prevent it from dominating us. Intellectually we know we should live in the present moment. Yet we're always being pushed by our habit energy of rushing around. We've lost our capacity to be in the present moment. This is why *practicing* mindfulness and concentration is so important; talking and reading about it is not enough.

LOOKING DEEPLY

In meditation, we practice concentration, bringing everything into sharp, clear focus. This is called *one-pointedness of mind*. Only when there is concentration can the work of looking deeply take place. We use our breathing to bring all the energy of our mind consciousness to one point. Our confusion stops, and we are able to sustain the energy of our mind consciousness on one object. The object of our concentration—the queen bee around which our swarming thoughts can gather—may be our breathing, a leaf, a pebble, a flower, a situation we are in, a person we want to understand better, or whatever else we want to make the object of our meditative focus. It's like putting a spotlight on the object of our concentration. Just as when a performer is on stage and the spotlight is focused only on them, we focus our mind intently on the object of our concentration. When we use a lens to focus sunlight on one point, its energy is concentrated so effectively that we can burn a hole in a piece of cloth. In the same way, we focus our mind consciousness on one point, on one object, in order to get a breakthrough and understand it better.

ORANGE MEDITATION

When you eat an orange, make the eating into a meditation. Sit in a way that you feel comfortable and solid. Look at the orange in such a way that you can see the orange as a miracle. An orange is not something less than a miracle.

Hold the orange in the palm of your hand, look at it and smile. You see the orange tree, the orange blossom, you see the sun entering the leaves and the rain penetrating the ground beneath, and you see the tiny fruit form; and now the fruit has grown into a beautiful orange. So just looking and smiling to the orange, you get in touch with the wonders of life, because an orange is a wonder of life. Due to our lack of mindfulness and concentration we ignore this fact; we don't see that the orange in the palm of our hand is really a miracle. When you

look at the orange and smile to the orange,
you really see the orange in its splendor, in its
miraculous nature. And suddenly you yourself
become a miracle, because you *are* a miracle.
You are not something less than a miracle.
Your presence is a miracle. You are a miracle
encountering another miracle.

You peel the orange. You smell it, and
in you there is the element of solidity,
true presence, and awareness. Life in this
moment becomes something real, something
wonderful.

NEURAL PATHWAYS

Traced in your brain are many neural pathways
that can lead to suffering or happiness. You
may travel on some of them frequently and
they have become a habit, always leading you
to react in the same way. For example, when
you're in touch with a certain thing, perhaps a
memory or an object, it may always take you
down a pathway that leads to anger and hate.
With the practice of mindfulness, concentration, and insight, you can choose instead to
focus on something wholesome that leads you
to a feeling of happiness. Or when a situation
arises that always leads you to react in a way
that brings suffering, if you can bring in mindfulness, you can choose to respond in a way
that contains more clarity and understanding.
Doing this a few times, you begin to open up

a new neural pathway that leads to happiness and reconciliation.

Suppose someone says something that angers you and your habit is to say something back to punish them, even if you know it won't help. Mindfulness can help you not to respond too quickly. You can say to yourself, "Hello, my anger, you are my old friend. I know you are there. I will take good care of you." Recognizing and embracing your anger will help bring relief. Practicing mindfulness of compassion like this, directed toward yourself and toward the person you believe to be the cause of your anger, allows compassion and understanding to arise, and your suffering and anger can begin to melt away. You are able to see the suffering in the other person and you may even find something to say that will help them.

MENTAL FORMATIONS

To be aware of our mind means to be aware of
the "mental formations," our various states of
mind. A "formation" is anything that is made
of other elements. A flower is a formation, a
physical formation. It is made of sun, rain, soil,
seed, and so on. Our hand is a physiological
formation. Our anger is a mental formation;
mindfulness and concentration are also mental
formations. According to my tradition, there are
fifty-one mental formations. As a young novice,
I had to memorize all of them. It is important
that we train ourselves to recognize each
mental formation when it arises and to call it
by its name. Contemplating the mind means
contemplating the mental formations.

THE FIVE UNIVERSAL
MENTAL FORMATIONS

Of the fifty-one mental formations there are five *universal mental formations* that are operating all the time: contact, feeling, attention, perception, and volition. They form a sequence, with one mental formation leading to the next, and the whole process from contact to volition can take place in less than a second.

Contact occurs when a sense organ touches a sense object, for example when our eyes see a flower. Whether we're aware of it or not, our senses are always coming into contact with something. A contact may make an impression that is mild or strong. Only when the intensity of a contact is important enough will *attention* manifest. Contact also serves as the foundation for *feeling* to arise. Mindfulness can come in at any time. But if it can be brought in by this point, it can intervene in the process of perception, before the energies of perception and volition push you to respond out of habit.

Perception is the energy that recognizes the form and characteristics of the object of our attention and gives it a name, like leaf or mountain. We have a concept of what is there. But we have to be careful, because all of us are frequently victims of wrong perception. We see a rope and may think it's a snake. So whatever we touch with our mind, we should know first of all that it is the object of our perception, and that our perception may be erroneous. Mindfulness can help us avoid wrong perception.

Perceptions and feelings give rise to *volition*, the energy that pushes us to respond—to *do* something, to run toward or away from something. Sometimes you know that doing a certain thing may destroy you, yet you still want to do it, because your volition is so strong. With the intervention of mindfulness and concentration, you can have the insight and determination to say, "No," and you are free.

Our brain has neuroplasticity; it can change, and we can change. The five universal mental formations form a neural pathway that can take us to a habitual response or, with the intervention of mindfulness, concentration, and insight, can create a new neural pathway that leads to understanding and compassion, happiness and healing.

THE SECRET OF SUCCESS IN MEDITATION

The practice of non-thinking is the secret of success in meditation. When thinking settles in, you lose the first impression of contact and a chance to be in the here and the now, to be in touch with what's inside and around you. Instead, just become aware of contact and feelings. Then you can be in touch with the elements of nourishment and healing available in your body and the environment, both physical and mental. When the feeling is pleasant, stop all thinking and just become aware of the feeling. It may be the pleasant feeling of walking barefoot on the beach. Walking on the beach, you can be very happy if you are able to let go of thinking of this or that. Brushing your teeth, going to the toilet, turning on the light or the water tap, any moment can be a moment of happiness.

SAVORING A BEAN CAKE

When I was four or five years old, every time
my mother went to the market, she brought me
back a cake made of bean paste. While she
was away, I would be playing in the garden
with the snails and the pebbles, and when my
mother came back I was very happy to see her.
I took the cake that she gave me and I went
off to eat it in the garden. I knew I mustn't eat
it quickly. I wanted to eat it slowly—the slower
the better. I'd just chew a little bit off the edge
to allow the sweetness of the cake to go into
my mouth, and I'd look up at the blue sky. I'd
look down at the dog. I'd look at the cat. That
is how I ate the cake, and it would take me
half an hour to eat it. I had no worries; I wasn't
thinking about fame, honor, or profit, the past
or the future. All of us have lived moments like

that, when we're not craving for anything, not regretting anything. We're not asking ourselves philosophical questions like "Who am I?" Are we able to eat a cake like that now?

THIS IS IT

The opportunity that you have been waiting for
is right here in the present moment.

Each step is that opportunity; each breath
is that opportunity—an opportunity for you
to go back to the now and stop your endless
wandering and waiting for that day to come.

The day that you've been waiting for is today;
the moment that you've been waiting for
is this very moment.

You must pierce the veil of time and space in
order to come to the here and the now.

No matter what your circumstances are, that
opportunity is there for you. In the now, you will
find what you have been looking for.

BE THE SOVEREIGN OF
YOUR TERRITORY

Imagine there's a country that doesn't have a government, a king, a queen, or a president. There is nobody around to take care of the country. The country needs a government. It's the same with ourselves. We need to be present in our territory, to take care of it, because our territory is large—it includes our body, feelings, perceptions, mental formations, and consciousness. We need to be the king or queen and govern our territory. We need to know what is precious and beautiful so we can protect it. We need to know what things aren't so beautiful so we can fix or transform them. We need to be a good queen or king and not run away from our country.

There are people who don't want to be the king or queen, who just want to run away from the job because they think it's so tiring. We run away by watching television, eating something, using social media, checking our email or the news, playing video games, listening to music, or socializing in various ways. We don't want to return to our homeland. As kings and queens we need to become aware of our responsibility, to see that we need to be the sovereign, to return to our territory and take care of it. We can learn ways to do this. Practicing mindfulness and concentration, we know how to do it. All the essential methods are in the sixteen exercises of mindful breathing. [See the Practices section in the second part of the book.]

Be mindful of your breath and your steps so you can be truly present in every moment of your life and have sovereignty over your kingdom. Then when you want to speak or act, you'll express yourself mindfully, and you'll be able listen deeply and understand the difficulties and joys of another person.

CURIOSITY AND INVESTIGATION

If you want to succeed in the practice of concentration, make it interesting. If you are interested enough in the object of your focus, concentration will be easy, and it can touch the deepest level of your consciousness. Understanding is a fruit of mindfulness and concentration. If you are not interested in something, you can never understand it. If you are not interested in someone, you can never understand them. If you are interested in them deeply, you will be mindful and concentrated, and it will be easy to find out all about them. When you are interested in something, when it is important to you, everything becomes interesting—a leaf, a pebble, a cloud, a pond, a person, a situation, your child. You feel eager to look deeply into all of these things, to find out their true nature. When concentration becomes easy, natural, effortless, it is true concentration.

THE ULTIMATE DIMENSION

There are two dimensions to life, and we should be able to touch them both. One is like a wave, and we call it *the historical dimension*. The other is like the water, and we call it *the ultimate dimension*, or *nirvana*. We usually touch just the wave, but when we discover how to touch the water, we receive the highest fruit that meditation can offer.

In the historical dimension, we have birth certificates and death certificates. The day your mother passes away, you suffer. If someone sits close to you and shows concern, you feel some relief. This is the world of waves. It is characterized by birth and death, ups and downs, being and nonbeing. A wave has a beginning and an end, but we cannot ascribe these characteristics to water. In the world of water, there is no birth or death, no being or nonbeing, no beginning or end. When we touch the water, we touch reality in its ultimate dimension and are liberated from all of these concepts. If you know how to touch your mother in the ultimate dimension, she will always be with you; you can see that she is there in you, smiling. This is a deep practice and it is also the deepest kind of relief.

One day as I was about to step on a dry leaf, I saw the leaf in the ultimate dimension. I saw that it was not really dead, but it was merging with the moist soil and preparing to appear on the tree the following spring in another form. I smiled to the leaf and said, "You are pretending." Everything is pretending to be born and pretending to die, including the leaf I almost stepped on. The day of our so-called death is a day of our continuation in many other forms.

LOOKING DEEPLY INTO THE NATURE OF REALITY

Unlike scientists, spiritual practitioners don't use sophisticated research instruments. They use their inner wisdom—their luminosity—to look into things. Once we get rid of our grasping, our fear and anger, our notions and concepts, then we have a very bright instrument with which to experience reality free from dualistic notions of birth and death, being and nonbeing, coming and going, the same or different. The practice of mindfulness, concentration, and insight can purify our mind and make it into a powerful instrument with which we can look deeply into the nature of reality.

THINKING GLOBALLY

We may feel that we are not capable of touching the ultimate dimension but that isn't correct. We have done it already. The problem is how to do it more deeply and more frequently. The phrase "Think globally," for example, is in the direction of touching the ultimate dimension. When we see things globally, we avoid many mistakes and we have a more profound view of happiness and life. The spot you are standing on includes the whole earth. When you practice walking meditation, you realize that with each step you take, you are touching the whole earth. When you touch one thing with deep awareness, you touch everything. The same is true of time. When you touch one moment with deep awareness, you touch all moments. If you live one moment deeply, that moment contains all the past and all the future in it. When you drink a cup of tea very deeply, you touch the present moment and you touch the whole of time.

THE FOUR NUTRIMENTS

When something has come to be, we have to
acknowledge its presence and look deeply into
it to discover the kinds of nourishment that have
helped it come to be and continue to feed it.
Nothing can live without food; whether it's our
love, our hate, our thinking, our depression—it
can't continue without nourishment. It's
important that we can identify what we've been
ingesting that has fed and sustained our happiness and our suffering. There are four kinds of
nutriments that can bring about our happiness
or suffering: *edible food*, *sense impressions*,
volition, and *consciousness*. When we are able
to identify our suffering and see its causes,
we will have more peace and joy, and we are
already on the path to liberation.

EDIBLE FOOD

It's important that we learn ways to shop, cook, and eat that preserve the health and well-being of our body and our spirit. We eat only the things that can bring peace and well-being into our body and mind. We eat in a way that helps retain compassion in our heart. We have to look deeply to see how we grow our food, so we can eat in ways that preserve our collective well-being, minimize our suffering and the suffering of other species, and allow the earth to continue to be a source of life for all of us, assuring a future for our children.

SENSE IMPRESSIONS

Our six sense organs—eyes, ears, nose, tongue, body, and mind—are in constant contact with sense objects, and these contacts become food for our consciousness. When we drive through a city, our eyes see many billboards and these images enter our consciousness. When we pick up a magazine, the articles and advertisements are food for our consciousness. Not only children need to be protected from violent and unwholesome programs, films, books, magazines, games, and social media. We, too, can be destroyed by these things. If we are mindful, we will know whether we are ingesting toxins or nourishing ourselves with sense impressions that encourage understanding, compassion, and the determination to help others.

VOLITION

Volition, our deepest desire or intention, is
the ground of all our actions. We have to ask
ourselves, "What is my deepest desire in this
life?" Our desire can take us in the direction of
happiness or suffering. Desire is a kind of food
that nourishes and gives us energy. If you have
a healthy desire, such as a wish to protect life
and the environment or to live a simple life with
time to take care of yourself and your beloved
ones, your desire will bring you to happiness.
If you run after power, wealth, sex, and fame,
thinking that they will bring you happiness, you
are consuming a very dangerous kind of food
that will bring you a lot of suffering. You can
see this is true just by looking around you. For
example, if you think that becoming president
of a large corporation is what will make you

happy, everything you do or say will be directed toward realizing that goal. Even when you sleep, your consciousness will continue to work on it. Or perhaps we believe that our suffering and that of our family has been brought about by someone who wronged us in the past. We feel we will only be happy if we can hurt that person, so our life is motivated solely by the desire for revenge and punishment.

Everyone wants to be happy, and there is a strong energy inside us pushing us toward what we think will make us happy. We need to see that position, wealth, fame, possessions, or revenge are often the very obstacles to our happiness. We can cultivate our wish to be free of these things and nourish our deepest desire so we can enjoy the wonders of life that are always available—the blue sky, the trees, our beautiful children.

CONSCIOUSNESS

If we have not been able to transform the painful events of our past, then they are still buried in our consciousness. When we allow painful images from the past to come up, it's like we are eating our own consciousness; and the more we think, the more angry and upset we become. We chew our suffering and despair like cows chew their cud. We ruminate on our suffering and we suffer all over again. But in our consciousness, there are also the seeds of enlightenment. Our consciousness has as many channels as a television. Why don't we push the button of compassion and understanding and change the channel?

We consume our own individual consciousness and we consume the collective consciousness. In both there are nourishing

foods and toxic foods. We should be aware
that when we spend time close to a community
that has a great deal of hatred and despair,
these energies will penetrate into us. We
need to find a collective environment that is
nourishing, where the people are motivated by
compassion and helping others.

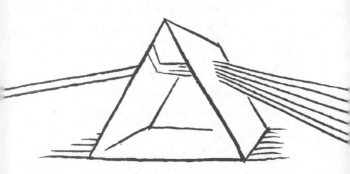

THE PEUGEOT

In the 1970s, within a few years of arriving
in France, our group bought a little car—a
secondhand Peugeot. We went all over Europe
in it and used the car to transport not only
people but also sand, bricks, tools, books,
food, and many other materials as we began to
establish the Sweet Potato community in an old
farmhouse outside Paris. We used it for all our
needs and kept it for many years. When our car
was old and couldn't be used anymore, we had
a difficult time letting it go. We were attached
to our little Peugeot, because both we and
the car had gone through so much together.
The car had survived breakdowns, numerous
accidents, and untold repairs. My friends and
I were sad the night we had to abandon it.

I don't know if people develop such a deep connection to the things they buy these days. Many people have a strong desire to possess the latest thing, and manufacturers and advertisers know this. It is not by accident that merchandise is not created to last. The objects of our desire are constantly changing. And our desires for the objects we consume also change from one moment to the next. We are always running after something new. We may be infatuated with what we've bought for a while, but soon we take it for granted, we get bored, throw it away, and then buy something else. As you grow in mindfulness and concentration, you reclaim your life. You begin to see how much time we lose in empty, meaningless consumption. Looking deeply, we see that running after such objects of desire brings us no lasting happiness, only suffering.

MAINTAINING MOTIVATION

When we're not in touch with our volition, our deepest desire, then even if we struggle and try hard, concentration will not come easily. When that desire is strong in us, the concentration needed to realize real awakening arises effortlessly. Whether we are eating, drinking, walking, or washing dishes, even when we think we're not very concentrated, we *are* concentrated because we are being motivated by that strong desire. Scientists and philosophers who are concentrated on their special subjects also have this kind of desire. When we touch our deepest desire, concentration comes easily and stays with us for a long time. We will be in constant concentration, not only in the meditation hall, but in the bathroom, the garden, the kitchen, the market, wherever we go.

THE SPIRITUAL IS IN
THE ORDINARY

With mindfulness and concentration, everything becomes spiritual. Where do you seek the spiritual? Seek it in every ordinary thing that you do every day. Sweeping the floor, watering the vegetables, and washing the dishes become holy and sacred if mindfulness and concentration are there. Every minute can be a holy, sacred minute.

Washing dishes in the historical dimension,
I see them piled high.
Looking from the ultimate dimension.
The pile presents no obstacle.

LIKE A CLEAR MOUNTAIN LAKE

Near the mountain, there is a lake with clear, still water reflecting the mountain and the sky with pristine clarity. You can do the same. If you are calm and still enough, you can reflect the mountain, the blue sky, and the moon exactly as they are. You reflect whatever you see exactly as it is, without distorting anything. Sitting quietly, just breathing in and out, we develop concentration, clarity, and strength. So sit like a mountain. No wind can blow the mountain down. If you can sit for half an hour, enjoy sitting for half an hour. If you can sit for a few minutes, enjoy sitting for a few minutes. That is also good.

ONE THING AT A TIME

Each morning at work you may get a lot of important emails, and you have to decide which one to read first. There may be two that seem to be equally important, but you have to choose one. After making that decision, you should be only with that email. When you are crossing a bridge, you just cross that bridge. Don't think of the next bridge. You will have to cross it, but only after you have crossed this one. This is our practice, this is concentration: one-pointed mind. If we haven't trained ourselves in bringing all our attention to just one object, there will be dispersion and disturbance. This is a question of training. You have to be 100 percent with what is there in the here and the now; concentration is essential.

If you are a therapist, you do the same. When you are with one patient, don't think of the other patients. You have to focus 100 percent of your mind on this one, and to be with them entirely. Maybe you have the desire to do many things, to help many people. The Buddha also had the desire to help many people. But he was capable of being fully present with one person, in order to understand them deeply enough that he could offer them the best teaching and solution. So we, as a teacher, as a therapist, as a parent, have to practice the same way, focusing our attention on one object in the here and the now.

RIGHT VIEW

We practice mindfulness and concentration
to get Right View. Otherwise our view will not
be in accord with reality—it will not have the
wisdom of impermanence, nonself, nondiscrimination, and interbeing—and therefore
our thinking, speech, and actions will produce
suffering for ourselves and others. Until we can
see clearly, our wrong perceptions will keep
us from having Right View. Touching reality
deeply is the way to liberate ourselves from
wrong perceptions. When we have the foundation of Right View, every thought, word, and
deed we produce can be in line with the insight
of Right View. There are many practices of
concentration that can help us cultivate Right
View. Right View is the insight we have into the
reality of life.

THE THREE DHARMA SEALS

The Three Dharma Seals are three concentrations: on impermanence, nonself, and nirvana. They are the mark of every Buddhist teaching and are the keys to touching every phenomenon deeply and opening the door of reality. Mindfulness and concentration are the energies we can use to be in touch with something. When we are in touch with our heart, for example, our heart feels this and is very happy to receive our attention. If we use our mindfulness to touch it deeply enough, we see its *impermanent* nature. Even if our heart was healthy three months ago, that doesn't guarantee it will be in good health forever, especially if we don't look after it and take care of it. At the same time, we see the *nonself*, interdependent nature of our heart. The well-being of our heart depends on many other elements, like the health of our other organs, the things we eat and drink, our environment, and hereditary factors.

When we look deeply into the impermanent and nonself nature of our heart, we begin to understand the difficulties it has. We feel love and wish to care for it, and our way of acting can transform the state of our heart. The same applies to every other part of our body. We stop smoking, eating, and drinking in ways that cause our liver to be exhausted, our lungs to malfunction, or the flow of blood to and from our heart to be constricted. When we use the Three Dharma Seals as a key to open the door to the reality of our body, we come to understand it deeply. Only once we understand it deeply will we look after it carefully.

In the same way, we can use these three keys to open the door to the reality of all phenomena. Impermanence and nonself belong to the world of phenomena, the historical dimension. When we touch phenomena deeply, looking at the world in terms of impermanence and nonself, then we are in the sphere of *nirvana*, the ultimate dimension, and we feel at ease and without fear. Impermanence and nonself are in essence the same; they both mean the absence of a separate, permanent self. It is called impermanence when looked at in terms of time, and nonself when looked at in terms of space. Our store consciousness, our unconscious mind, is impermanent and without a separate self, and—just like a flower or a piece of bread—it contains within itself all phenomena in the cosmos.

IMPERMANENCE

Intellectually we know that everything is impermanent, but in our daily life we still behave as if things are permanent. Impermanence is more than an idea. It is a practice to help us touch reality. Every time we look or listen, the object of our perception can reveal to us the nature of impermanence. We can nourish our insight into impermanence all day long. When we look deeply into impermanence, we see that things change because causes and conditions change.

We need to learn to appreciate the value of impermanence. If we are in good health and are aware of impermanence, we will take good care of ourselves. When we know that the person we love is impermanent, we will cherish our beloved all the more. Impermanence teaches us to respect and value every moment and all the precious things around us and inside us. When we practice mindfulness of impermanence, we don't take things for granted and we become more present, more loving, and we see everything with fresh eyes.

Looking deeply can become a way of life. We can practice conscious breathing to help us be in touch with things and look deeply at their impermanent nature. This practice will keep us from complaining that everything is impermanent. Impermanence is what makes transformation possible. Thanks to impermanence, we can change suffering into joy. When we practice the art of mindful living, then when things change, we won't have any regrets.

We have to nourish our insight into impermanence every day. If we do, we will live more deeply, suffer less, and enjoy life much more. Living deeply, we will touch the foundation of reality: nirvana, the world of no birth and no death. Touching impermanence deeply, we touch the world beyond permanence and impermanence. We touch the ground of being and see that what we have called being and nonbeing are just notions. Nothing is ever lost. Nothing is ever gained.

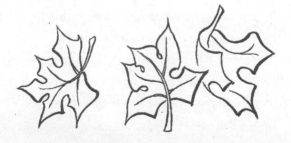

PRACTICING THE INSIGHT OF IMPERMANENCE

Suppose you're angry with your partner. They just said something that made you suffer deeply. You're suffering so much that you have a desire to say something back to make them suffer. You believe that by doing this, you will suffer less. We're intelligent enough to know that this is childish behavior, but many of us still do it anyway. If you say something that makes the other person suffer, then they'll try to get relief by saying something back to make you suffer. Both of you are practicing the escalation of anger. Suppose instead you practice the concentration on impermanence. You just close your eyes and breathe in. In the three or four seconds of breathing in, you visualize how your loved one will be three hundred years from now.

What will my loved one be three hundred
   years from now?
What will I be three hundred years from now?

The concentration on impermanence brings you the insight right away that your loved one is impermanent, that you are impermanent, and that it's silly to make each other suffer like this in the present moment. The concentration on impermanence will bring the insight of imper-manence, allowing you to touch in a very real way the nature of impermanence in yourself and your loved one. When you open your eyes, you're so happy that they are still alive, the only thing you want to do is open your arms and hug them.

Breathing in, darling, I know you are still alive.
Breathing out, I am so happy.

NONSELF

When we look deeply into anything, we see that its existence is possible only because of the existence of everything else. From the point of view of time, we say *impermanence,* and from the point of view of space, we say *nonself.* Things cannot remain themselves for two consecutive moments; therefore, there is nothing that can be called a permanent self. From one moment to the next, you are different physically and mentally. Looking deeply at impermanence, you see nonself. Looking deeply at nonself, you see impermanence. We see that we are made of non-us elements, and in us we can recognize ancestors, parents, cultures, society—everything. This teaching can be made simple enough that children, too, can understand it. For example, we can visualize the family element in us:

Within me I see my father as a five-year-old child,
small and vulnerable.
I smile to him with compassion.

Such a guided meditation can help us touch the truth of nonself. When you know you are made of non-you elements, you know that your father is in you, fully alive in every cell of your body, and his suffering is still there in you. This kind of practice can bring the insight of interbeing and nonself. It can liberate you from any anger you have toward him.

Insight brings love, and love isn't possible without insight. If you don't understand, you can't love. This is insight, direct understanding, and not just an idea. In meditation we allow the light of that insight to shine on us. Nothing has a separate existence, a separate self. Everything has to inter-be with everything else.

NONSELF COOKIES

The first time I ever tasted peanut butter cookies, I loved them! I was at Tassajara Zen Mountain Center in California. I learned that you mix the ingredients to prepare the batter, and then you put each cookie onto a cookie sheet using a spoon. I imagined that the moment each cookie leaves the bowl of dough and is placed onto the tray, it begins to think of itself as separate. You, the creator of the cookies, know better, and you have a lot of compassion for them. You know that they are originally all one and that, even now, the happiness of each cookie is still the happiness of all the other cookies. But they have developed discriminative perception, and suddenly they set up barriers between themselves. When you put them in the oven, they begin to talk to each other: "Get out of my way. I want to be in the middle." "I am brown and beautiful, and you are ugly!" "Can't you please spread a little in that direction?" We have the tendency to behave this way too, and it causes a lot of suffering. If we know how to touch our nondiscriminating mind, our happiness and the happiness of others will increase many fold.

We all have the capacity of living with the wisdom of nondiscrimination, but we have to train ourselves to see in that way, to see that the flower is us, the mountain is us, our parents and our children are all us. When we see that everyone and everything belongs to the same stream of life, our suffering will vanish. Nonself is not a doctrine nor a philosophy, but an insight that can help us live life more deeply, suffer less, and enjoy life much more.

NIRVANA

When we understand impermanence and
nonself, we are already in touch with nirvana.
Many people think that nirvana is a place of
happiness where people who are enlightened
go when they die. No idea could be more
misleading. Nirvana can be realized right
here and right now, in this very life. Nirvana
means liberation and freedom. If we are able
to free ourselves from our afflictions such as
attachment, hatred, and jealousy, and we can
free ourselves from wrong views like our ideas
about birth and death, being and nonbeing,
coming and going, self and other, same and
different, we can be in touch with nirvana in the
present moment.

Nirvana cannot be described in words and concepts because it lies outside our language and notions. Nirvana means taking the time to enjoy where we are. The happiness that comes with nirvana is very great. If we want to enjoy nirvana, we have to abandon all the things that bind us in our everyday life, and quite automatically nirvana is there. It is the same as when we abandon our warm blankets and our idleness, open the door, and step outside. Immediately the cool breeze, the moon, and the stars are there for us. Do not wish for anything less than this.

PRACTICES FOR
DEVELOPING
CONCENTRATION

THE SIXTEEN EXERCISES OF MINDFUL BREATHING

In the Sutra on the Full Awareness of Breathing, the Buddha shows us how to develop our concentration and transform our fear, despair, anger, and craving. I was so happy the day I discovered this text. I thought I'd discovered the greatest treasure in the world. Before, I'd been content to simply gain knowledge. I didn't know how to enjoy the present moment, to look deeply into my life, and to enjoy the positive conditions that were all around me. This sutra is so basic and so wonderful. There are many great sutras, but approaching them without this one is like trying to reach the top of a mountain without a path to go on.

There are four sets of four exercises. The first set is for looking into the realm of the body. The second set is for looking into our feelings. The third set is to contemplate our mind. The fourth set is to contemplate the objects of our mind: all phenomena.

THE REALM OF THE BODY

The first four exercises help us return to our body in order to look deeply into it and care for it. The first object of awareness is our breath itself. Our breath may be short, long, heavy, or light. Just notice it; don't try to change it. Allow it to be. Practicing awareness in this way, our mind and our breath become one. We also see that breathing is an aspect of the body and that awareness of breathing puts us in touch with the body. It's important that in our daily life, we learn to create harmony and ease in our body and reunite body and mind. We breathe in and out with awareness and bring our mind back to our body. We focus on our body to calm, relax, heal, and bring ease to the body.

1 AWARENESS OF BREATHING

The first exercise is to be aware of your in-breath and out-breath. As you breathe in, bring your attention to your in-breath. Focus your attention only on your in-breath and release everything else—the past, the future, your projects. Just by breathing in, you are free, because in that moment you are not your sorrow, your fear, or your regret. You are only your in-breath. As you breathe in, say the first sentence silently; as you breathe out say the second sentence. As you continue to breathe in and out, you can use just the key words "in, out."

Breathing in, I know I'm breathing in.
Breathing out, I know I'm breathing out.
In.
Out.

Practicing this exercise is already enlightenment. Normally we don't know we're breathing
in. Now, we put our mind into it, and we recognize "I'm breathing in." We may have the insight,
"I'm alive"! To be alive is something wonderful.
Breathing in and breathing out in awareness can
be very enjoyable. This is the basis of mindfulness practice. Please don't underestimate
this easy exercise. Even if you've practiced
mindful breathing for many years, this remains a
wonderful practice, and you can continue to get
more and more benefit from it.

2 FOLLOWING THE BREATH

Breathing in, I follow my in-breath from
   the beginning to the end.
Breathing out, I follow my out-breath from
   the beginning to the end.
Following the in-breath.
Following the out-breath.

There's no interruption in your attention during the whole time of breathing in and breathing out. You focus your mind entirely on your in-breath and out-breath. Not a millisecond is lost. The object of your concentration is your in-breath. You are entirely with your in-breath, and you dwell very solidly in your in-breath. There's no more thinking, no more past, no more future. You're really enjoying your in-breath. You don't have to suffer during the practice. When you focus your attention on your breath, you will find out very quickly that you're a living reality, present here and now, sitting on this beautiful planet Earth, and around you there are trees, sunshine, and blue sky. When you practice mindful breathing while walking, you see that it's a wonder to be alive and making steps on this beautiful planet, and happiness comes right away.

3 AWARENESS OF BODY

Breathing in, I'm aware of my whole body.
Breathing out, I'm aware of my whole body.

We see that awareness of our breathing is, at the same time, awareness of our entire body. Our mind, our breath, and our whole body are one. We reconnect with our body. We remember our body is there. When body and mind are together we are truly present and we can live every moment of daily life deeply. We reconcile with our body, we become our body, and we stop the alienation and separation of body and mind from each other. Going back to your body, you touch the wonder that is the body. Its functioning is the result of millions of processes. If you know how to connect and be in touch with your body, you can connect with Mother Earth and the whole cosmos.

4 CALMING AND RELEASING TENSION IN THE BODY

Breathing in, I calm my body.
Breathing out, I release the tension in my body.

Calming our body allows it to rest. Resting is a precondition for the healing of body and mind. Returning to our body, we may become aware of the suffering and tension in our body. Living in forgetfulness, we've allowed stress and pain to accumulate in our body, and modern life brings added stress. We have to be kind to our body and give it an opportunity to relax. While breathing in and breathing out, we calm our body and allow the tension in our body to be released.

Whatever the position of our body, whether we're lying, standing, sitting, or walking, we can always practice mindful breathing and releasing the tension. You can practice while cooking breakfast, taking a shower, driving the car, or sitting on the bus. You don't have to set aside a special time. We shouldn't say, "I have no time to practice." We have plenty of time. We can practice all day long and get the benefit of practice right away.

Walking to the classroom, the workplace, or the meditation hall, you can allow the tension to be released with each step. Walk as a free person and enjoy every step you make. You're no longer in a hurry. Walk with ease, releasing the tension in the body with each step. This is the way to walk every time you need to go from one place to another. When you practice like this you get relaxation and joy, and it benefits everyone around you. To practice mindful breathing is an act of love. You become an instrument of peace and joy, and you can help others.

THE REALM OF THE FEELINGS

With these four exercises, we return to our feelings in order to develop joy and happiness and transform suffering. Our feelings are us. If we don't look after them, who will? Every day we have painful feelings, and we need to learn how to look after them. Our teachers and friends can help us to a certain extent, but we have to do the work. Our body and our feelings are our territory, and we are the king or queen responsible for that territory. After breathing with awareness and calming the body, it's natural for feelings of joy and well-being to arise. As you do the sixteen exercises, you will find that each exercise leads to the next.

5   CULTIVATING JOY

Breathing in, I'm aware of a feeling of joy.
Breathing out, I'm aware of a feeling of joy.

We tend to lose ourselves in our work and in our worries, and we can't see the wonders of life. Now we're coming back to be in touch with the clear air, the cup of tea, the flowers and grass, with the wonderful planet earth. We see that our senses allow us to be in touch with these things, and joy comes easily.

6   CULTIVATING HAPPINESS

Breathing in, I'm aware of a feeling of happiness.
Breathing out, I'm aware of a feeling of happiness.

In the sixth exercise, joy becomes happiness and peace. Happiness is possible here and now. We need only to breathe in for a few seconds to see that it's possible to be happy right away. Many people believe that wealth, power, or fame will make them happy. But by practicing this way we know that mindfulness and concentration are sources of happiness. Joy and happiness differ a little in that joy still contains some amount of excitement.

We tend to believe that we don't have enough conditions to be happy. We run into the future and look for more conditions of happiness. If we've mastered the first four exercises and find ourselves established in the here and the now, it's easy to recognize that we already have more than enough conditions to be happy. "Breathing in, I'm aware of the feeling of happiness" is not imagination or wishful thinking, because when we come back to ourselves, we can be in touch with the conditions for happiness within us and around us.

7 RECOGNIZING PAINFUL FEELINGS

Breathing in, I'm aware of a painful feeling in me.
Breathing out, I'm aware of a painful feeling in me.

This is the practice of simple recognition of the painful feeling that's arising. There is the energy of pain, but there is also the energy of mindfulness that is recognizing and embracing the pain tenderly, without the desire to suppress it. When we don't practice, it's easy to allow the pain to overwhelm us or to try to run away and cover up the painful feeling by eating, listening to music, going online— anything not to confront the suffering inside. The market provides us with many things to cover up our suffering. By consuming, we allow the suffering to grow. We have to be in touch with our pain in order to have an opportunity to heal it. We practice meditation to get in touch with our joy and happiness *and* with our suffering and pain. Bringing our mind back to our body and cultivating joy and happiness can give us the strength we need to encounter and embrace our painful feelings. We aren't running away or covering up anymore. Taking care of the painful feeling, our body and mind are no longer alienated from each other.

8   RELIEVING A PAINFUL FEELING

Breathing in, I embrace my painful feeling.
Breathing out, I calm my painful feeling.

When we know how to tenderly embrace a painful feeling or emotion, we can already get some relief. Every time we notice that a painful feeling or emotion is coming up, we come back to our mindful breathing and generate the energy of mindfulness and concentration to recognize and embrace the pain, in the same way that a loving mother recognizes the suffering of her child and embraces the child lovingly in her arms.

With these exercises for the feelings, we know how to handle happiness and pain. When we know how to handle happiness, we can continue to nourish our love, peace, and happiness with our awareness and keep them there for a long time. When there's pain, we're not afraid because we know how to handle it, get relief, and transform the pain into greater understanding. In the beginning we may not know where our suffering has come from, but if we're able to recognize it and hold it tenderly, we suffer less already. If we continue with mindfulness and concentration, we'll soon discover the source and the roots of our pain and suffering, and understanding and compassion can arise.

THE REALM OF THE MIND

The mind is made up of mental formations.
Each mental formation is like a drop of water in
the river of the mind. Anger, fear, mindfulness,
concentration, loving kindness, and insight are
all mental formations. In the ninth exercise of
mindful breathing, we sit on the bank of the
river of mental formations and recognize any
mental formation that arises.

9 AWARE OF MENTAL FORMATIONS

Breathing in, I contemplate my mind
Breathing out, I contemplate my mind.

All the mental formations can manifest in
mind consciousness. There are fifty-one
categories of mental formations: five universal,
five particular, eleven wholesome, twenty-six

unwholesome, and four indeterminate. First there are the five mental formations that are called universal because they operate at all times and in all levels of consciousness. The five particular do not operate with every consciousness. The category of wholesome mental formations includes compassion, loving kindness, faith, and so on. The category of unwholesome mental formations includes the major afflictions such as greed, anger, and delusion, and lesser unwholesome mental states such as vexation, selfishness, envy, and so on.

The indeterminate or neutral mental formations are neither inherently wholesome nor unwholesome. When our body and mind need rest, sleep is wholesome. But if we sleep too much it can be unwholesome. If we hurt someone and regret it, that is beneficial regret. But if our regret leads to a guilt complex that colors whatever we do in the future, it can be called unwholesome regret. When our thinking helps us see clearly it is beneficial. But if our mind is scattered in many directions, that thinking is unbeneficial.

All the mental formations are in our consciousness in the form of seeds. Every time one of them manifests as energy, we want to have enough awareness to recognize it and call it by its true name. "Hello there, my mental formation. Your name is jealousy. I know you. I will take good care of you."

The author has added a number of mental formations to the traditional list.

Five Universal Mental Formations

contact
attention
feeling
perception
volition

Five Particular Mental Formations

intention
determination
mindfulness
concentration
insight

Eleven Wholesome Mental Formations

faith
inner shame
shame before others
absence of craving
absence of hatred
absence of ignorance
diligence, energy
tranquility, ease
vigilance, energy
equanimity
non-harming

Wholesome Mental Formations Added by Thich Nhat Hanh

non-fear
absence of anxiety
stability, solidity
loving kindness
compassion
joy
humility
happiness
feverlessness
freedom, sovereignty

Six Primary Unwholesome Mental Formations

craving, covetousness
hatred
ignorance, confusion
arrogance
doubt, suspicion
wrong view

Twenty Secondary Unwholesome Mental Formations

anger
resentment, enmity
concealment
maliciousness
jealousy
selfishness, parsimony
deceitfulness, fraud
guile
desire to harm
mischievous
   exhuberance
lack of inner shame
lack of shame
   before others
restlessness
drowsiness
lack of faith, unbelief
laziness
negligence
forgetfulness
distraction
lack of discernment

Unwholesome Mental Formations Added by Thich Nhat Hanh

fear
anxiety
despair

Four Indeterminate Mental Formations (Neither Wholesome nor Unwholesome)

regret, repentance
sleepiness
initial thought
sustained thought

10 GLADDENING THE MIND

Breathing in, I make my mind happy.
Breathing out, I make my mind happy.

It's easier for the mind to become concentrated when it's in a peaceful, happy state than when it's filled with sorrow or anxiety. We are aware that we have the opportunity to practice meditation and that there is no moment as important as the present one. Calmly abiding in the present moment, joy arises each time we touch in ourselves the seeds of compassion, faith, goodness, equanimity, liberty, love, for-giveness, understanding, and so on. We know these mental formations are buried deep in our consciousness as seeds, and we need only touch them and water them with conscious breathing for them to manifest. In our daily life we should be able to nourish them and give them a chance to manifest as beautiful mental formations. Whenever the mental formation of compassion or joy arises, we feel wonderful. We have many good mental formations like this in our consciousness, and we should give them a chance to manifest as often as possible.

We know that our loved one also has good things inside, and we may like to say or do something to help these good things come up and make our loved one happy. You don't want to water the seeds of anger, fear, and jealousy in them. You only want to water the seeds of joy, happiness, and compassion in yourself and in the other person. This is called the practice of selective watering or Right Diligence. This strengthens our mind so that when we want to embrace and look into our negative mental formations, we're able to do so with more clarity and solidity.

11 CONCENTRATION

Breathing in, I concentrate my mind.
Breathing out, I concentrate my mind.

To meditate means to be fully present and to concentrate on the object of your meditation. All mental formations that manifest in the present moment can become objects of your concentration. You focus your mind wholly on one object, like a lens receiving rays of sunlight and concentrating them so they converge on one spot. In this way you can make a breakthrough into the true nature of the object of your meditation, and get the kind of insight, the kind of view that contains understanding and that will help liberate you from the things that bind you: your anger, craving, and delusion.

12 LIBERATION

Breathing in, I liberate my mind.
Breathing out, I liberate my mind.

Happiness is possible when we are liberated
from our anger, fear, and delusion. With the
eighth exercise, you can get some relief, but
our mind may still be bound by the past, the
future, latent desires, anger, and other afflictions. With clear observation, we can locate the
knots that are binding us and making it impossible for our mind to be free and at peace. We
loosen these knots and untie the ropes that
bind our mind. With full awareness of breathing
the light of observation shines in, illuminates
the mind, and sets it free. Looking deeply into
the nature of mental formations like fear, anger,
or anxiety brings about the understanding that
will liberate us from the causes of our suffering—attachment, violence, and delusion.

THE REALM OF THE OBJECTS
OF MIND

The last four exercises of mindful breathing offer
us some practices of concentration that can
help liberate us from the misperceptions and
delusion that have perpetuated our suffering.

Mind and object of mind arise at the same
time; mind and its object are always together.
Consciousness is always consciousness
of something. Feeling is always feeling
something. Loving and hating are always
loving and hating something. All physiological
phenomena, such as the breath, the nervous
system, and the sense organs; all psychologi-
cal phenomena, such as feelings, thoughts,
and consciousness; and all physical phenomena, such as the earth, water, grass, trees,
mountains, and rivers, are objects of mind. The
realm of the objects of mind is the realm of
perception.

13 IMPERMANENCE

Breathing in, I observe the impermanent nature
  of all things.
Breathing out, I contemplate the impermanent nature
  of all things.

The thirteenth breathing exercise sheds light
on the ever-changing, impermanent nature
of all that exists. Our breathing itself is also
impermanent. The insight into impermanence
opens the way for us to see the interrelated
and selfless nature of all that exists. Nothing
has a separate, independent self.

The contemplation on impermanence
can help us live our life with the insight of
impermanence so we can be free from many
afflictions such as anger, fear, and delusion.
It isn't the idea or notion of impermanence,
but the insight of impermanence that can free

and save us. Impermanence is not a negative note in the song of life. If there were no impermanence, life would be impossible. Without impermanence how could your little girl grow up and become a young woman? Without impermanence how could you hope to transform your suffering? You can hope to transform your suffering because you know it is impermanent. So impermanence is something positive. We should say, "Long live impermanence!"

14 LETTING GO

Breathing in, I contemplate letting go.
Breathing out, I contemplate letting go.

This is the practice of releasing and letting go of our notions and ideas. Notions of birth and death, being and nonbeing, self and other, same and different are the foundation of our fear and anxiety. Letting go of these notions sets you free. You touch your true nature. We let go of our notions and we're in touch with reality. To live with a clear mind and to understand the deepest teachings of great spiritual teachers, we have to remove our dualistic way of thinking, the source of our misunderstanding and wrong perceptions. If we're caught in dualistic thinking, when we observe a father and son, we'll see them as two completely different people. But when we look deeply into the person of the son, we see the father in each cell of the son. If you get angry with your father, even if you don't want to have anything to do with him ever again, you can't remove your father from you. Your father is present in every cell of your body.

15 ABANDONING DESIRE

Breathing in, I observe the disappearance of desire.
Breathing out, I observe the disappearance of desire.

This exercise allows us to recognize the true
nature of the object of our desire, to see that
every phenomenon is impermanent, already in
the process of disintegrating, so that we are no
longer possessed by the idea of holding on to
anything as an object of our desire or seeing
it as a separate entity. When we breathe in
and look deeply into the object of our craving,
we see the many dangers hidden within it.
We know that running after it may destroy our
body and mind. We see many people destroy-
ing themselves by running after the object of
their craving. At the same time there are other
people who see that true happiness is made
of understanding and love. The more they

cultivate understanding and love, the happier they become. That is how contemplating non-craving helps us to be liberated. We look deeply to see the true nature of the object of our craving.

16   EXTINCTION OF ALL NOTIONS

Breathing in, I contemplate the extinction of all notions.
Breathing out, I contemplate the extinction of
  all notions.

Nirvana is our true nature of no birth and no death, no being and no nonbeing. Nirvana is insight, the freedom from all kinds of notions, concepts, ideas, and misperceptions. It's possible to touch our nature of nirvana during this very life. Nirvana is available in the here and the now. Many people in the Christian tradition use the beautiful phrase "resting in

God." Allowing yourself to rest in God is like a wave resting in its essential nature: the water. Imagine a wave rising and falling on the surface of the ocean. Observing the wave, we can see it has a beginning and an end; it comes up and it goes down. But when the wave looks into herself, she sees that she is water. She's a wave, but she is also water, and water cannot be described in terms of being and nonbeing, coming and going, up and down. The wave is water right in the here and now.

Just as the wave doesn't need to go looking for water, we don't need to go seeking nirvana. Nirvana is already there. We can enjoy nirvana right away. With mindfulness and concentration, we are able to touch our true nature. We know that a cloud can never die; it can only become snow, rain, or ice. A cloud can never become nothing. The true nature of no birth and no death is there in everything, including ourselves. To be the cloud floating in the sky is a wonderful thing, and to become the rain falling down on the Earth and nourishing everything is also a wonderful thing. To become a river, to become a cup of tea for someone to drink is also wonderful. To become water vapor and a cloud again is also something wonderful.

This insight corresponds to what science has found and expressed in the first law of thermodynamics: that nothing is born, nothing dies; everything is in transformation.

You can study and practice these sixteen exercises intelligently. The first four exercises help our concentration very much, and every time we practice it's helpful to do them. But it isn't always necessary to practice the sixteen exercises in sequence or to practice all sixteen in one session. For example, you might like to focus on practicing the fourteenth exercise for several days or longer. These exercises are presented very simply, but their effectiveness is immeasurable.

THE THREE DOORS
OF LIBERATION

To the practice of the Sixteen Exercises we can add the concentrations on The Three Doors of Liberation: emptiness, signlessness, and aimlessness. The teaching of the Three Doors of Liberation is found in all schools of Buddhism. Entering these doors, we dwell in concentration, in touch with reality and liberated from fear, confusion, and sadness.

EMPTINESS

Breathing in, I contemplate emptiness.
Breathing out, I contemplate emptiness.

Emptiness does not mean nonexistence. It means impermanence, nonself, interdependent co-arising—that is, that things arise depending on each other and are made of each other. The flower depends on the rain, the soil, and other elements, and the flower is full of everything in the cosmos—sunshine, clouds, air, and space. The flower is empty of only one thing: a separate existence. That is the meaning of emptiness. This concentration is a key to unlock the door to reality.

We maintain the awareness that everything is connected. Our happiness and suffering are the happiness and suffering of others. When our actions are based on nonself, they will be in accord with reality. We will know what to do and what not to do to help the situation. True emptiness goes beyond notions of existence and nonexistence, being and nonbeing. To say that the flower exists is not exactly correct, but to say that it does not exist is also not correct. Everything is in a state of constant change and is empty of a separate self. When we penetrate emptiness deeply, we see the interbeing nature of everything that is.

SIGNLESSNESS

Breathing in, I contemplate signlessness.
Breathing out, I contemplate signlessness.

"Sign" means a form, an appearance, an object of our perception. Everything manifests by means of signs, but we tend to get caught by these signs. If you see a flower only as a flower and don't see the sunshine, clouds, earth, time, and space in it, you are caught in the sign of the flower. When you touch the interbeing nature of the flower, however, you truly see the flower. If you see a person and don't also see their society, education, ancestors, culture, and environment, you have not really seen that person. Instead, you have been taken in by the sign of that person, the outward appearance of a separate self. When you can see that person deeply, you touch the whole cosmos, and you will not be fooled by appearances.

Until we touch the signless nature of things, we cannot touch reality. The greatest relief is when we break through the barriers of sign and touch the world of signlessness: nirvana. Where do we look to find the world of no signs? Right here in the world of signs. When we go beyond signs, we enter the world of nonduality, non-fear, and non-blaming. We can see the flower, the water, and our child beyond space and time. We know that our ancestors are present in us, right here and right now. We see that the Buddha, Jesus, Gandhi, Martin Luther King, Jr., and all our spiritual ancestors have not died.

AIMLESSNESS

Breathing in, I contemplate aimlessness.
Breathing out, I contemplate aimlessness.

There is nothing to do, nowhere to go, nothing to realize, nothing to attain. Does the rose have to *do* something? No, the purpose of a rose is to be a rose. Your purpose is to be yourself. You contain the whole cosmos. You don't have to run after anything or become someone else. You are wonderful just as you are. Aimlessness allows us to enjoy ourselves, the blue sky, and everything that is refreshing and healing in the present moment.

We don't need to put anything in front of us and run after it. We already have everything we are looking for. Life is precious as it is. All the elements for your happiness are already here. There is no need to run, strive, search, or struggle; just *be*. Simply being in the moment in this place is the deepest practice of meditation. Most people can't believe that just walking as though you have nowhere to go is enough. They think that striving and competing are normal and necessary. Try practicing aimlessness for just five minutes, and you will see how happy you are during those five minutes.

The moment of chopping wood and carrying water *is* the moment of happiness. We do not need to wait for these chores to be done to be happy. To have happiness in this moment is the spirit of aimlessness. Otherwise, we will run in circles for the rest of our lives. We have everything we need to make the present moment the happiest moment in our life, even if we have a headache or a cold, we don't have to wait. Having a cold is part of life.

We meditate not to attain enlightenment, because enlightenment is already there in us. We don't have to search anywhere. We don't need a purpose or a goal. We don't practice in order to obtain a high position. When we see that we don't lack anything, that we already are what we want to become, then our striving just comes to a halt. We are at peace in the present moment, just seeing the sunlight streaming through our window or hearing the sound of the rain. We don't have to run anywhere. We can enjoy every moment. People talk about entering nirvana, but we are already there. Aimlessness and nirvana are one. All we have to do is to be ourselves, fully and authentically. We simply return to ourselves and touch the peace and joy that are already there within and around us.

Related Titles by Thich Nhat Hanh

Be Free Where You Are

Breathe, You Are Alive!

Cultivating the Mind of Love

Happiness

The Heart of the Buddha's Teaching

How to Walk

Making Space

Old Path White Clouds

Present Moment, Wonderful Moment

Understanding Our Mind

Zen and the Art of Saving the Planet

Further Resources

For information about our international community, visit: plumvillage.org

To find an online sangha, visit: plumline.org

For more practices and resources, download the Plum Village app: plumvillage.app

Monastics and visitors practice the art of mindful living in the tradition of Thich Nhat Hanh at our mindfulness practice centers around the world. To reach any of these communities, or for information about how individuals, couples, and families can join in a retreat, please contact:

Plum Village
33580 Dieulivol, France
plumvillage.org

Magnolia Grove Monastery
Batesville, MS 38606, USA
magnoliagrovemonastery.org

Blue Cliff Monastery
Pine Bush, NY 12566, USA
bluecliffmonastery.org

Deer Park Monastery
Escondido, CA 92026, USA
deerparkmonastery.org

**European Institute of
Applied Buddhism**
D-51545 Waldbröl, Germany
eiab.eu

Thailand Plum Village
Nakhon Ratchasima
30130 Thailand
thaiplumvillage.org

Healing Spring Monastery
77510 Verdelot,
France
healingspringmonastery.org

Maison de l'Inspir
77510 Villeneuve-sur-Bellot
France
maisondelinspir.org

**Asian Institute of
Applied Buddhism**
Ngong Ping, Lantau Island
Hong Kong
pvfhk.org

**Nhap Luu-Stream
Entering Monastery**
Porcupine Ridge, Victoria 3461
Australia
nhapluu.org

Mountain Spring Monastery
Bilpin, Victoria 2758
Australia
mountainspringmonastery.org

The Mindfulness Bell, a journal of the art of mindful living in the tradition of Thich Nhat Hanh, is published two times a year by our community. To subscribe or to see the worldwide directory of sanghas (local mindfulness groups), visit **mindfulnessbell.org**.

**PARALLAX
PRESS**

Parallax Press, a nonprofit publisher founded
by Zen Master Thich Nhat Hanh, publishes
books and media on the art of mindful living
and Engaged Buddhism. We are committed to
offering teachings that help transform suffering
and injustice. Our aspiration is to contribute to
collective insight and awakening, bringing about a
more joyful, healthy, and compassionate society.

View our entire library at **parallax.org**.